To the Moon!

by Jesse McDermott
illustrated by Victor Kennedy

Editorial Offices: Glenview, Illinois • Parsippany, New Jersey • New York, New York
Sales Offices: Needham, Massachusetts • Duluth, Georgia • Glenview, Illinois
Coppell, Texas • Ontario, California • Mesa, Arizona

Paul, Wendy, and Tom were riding home on the bus with their science class. The class was studying gravity and the moon, and they had spent the whole day at the Science Museum with their teacher, Mr. Richards. Paul hadn't really understood gravity. How could you be weightless?

"I wish we could go to the moon!" Wendy exclaimed. Tom nodded in agreement.

What would it be like, Paul wondered, if all of them really could go to the moon?

He yawned. It was a long ride back to school.

Suddenly, Wendy started shaking Paul to awaken him. "Come on, we're here!" she cried. "We're at the spaceport and we're going to the moon!"

Paul blinked hard. Was this a dream? He pinched himself, but when he looked up, he saw a spaceport!

"We've all been chosen to go to the moon!" Tom said. "Isn't that great? Shhh, let's listen. The pilot's going to explain our trip now."

A man in a blue uniform strode to the front of the room. "Welcome, moon travelers!" he said. "I'm Pilot Jeffries. The first part of your trip is similar to flying in an airplane. You strap in with these two seat belts, which make an "X" on your chest." The screen zoomed in on a man strapped to a padded chair. "Then things get a little tricky," the pilot continued, chuckling.

Everything inside the spaceport loomed before Paul's eyes. It all looked so scary.

Paul swallowed so loudly he was sure his friends could hear. He wasn't sure he wanted to go to the moon! Was it safe? The pilot continued to describe what would happen on their trip to the moon.

"You look as though you'd rather be somewhere else," Wendy taunted. "You aren't scared, are you?"

"He said, 'things get tricky.'" Paul's voice wavered. "That doesn't scare you?"

"That sounds exciting!" Tom said.

"When you're told to get back to your seats, make sure you strap yourself in for our landing," the pilot finished his instructions. "OK, it's time to go!"

Most of the students cheered, but Paul was silent. If this was a dream, wasn't it time for him to wake up?

Summoning up his courage, Paul got in line behind Wendy. Any minute, he told himself, he'd wake up!

As the students began following Pilot Jeffries to the boarding platform, Paul staggered and stumbled. Luckily, Tom was right behind him, pushing him forward. Pilot Jeffries suddenly tapped Paul's shoulder.

"Have you ever flown before, son?" he asked.

"Once, and I got sick," Paul replied.

"Well, we certainly don't want that to happen on this flight!" Pilot Jeffries grinned. He looked through a small black bag at his side. He finally pulled out a small patch. He removed the backing and placed the patch behind Paul's ear.

"This will help," said Pilot Jeffries. "Nerves inside your ear tell your brain which way you're moving. Sometimes, what those nerves tell your brain and what your eyes see are two different things. That's when you get sick!"

The students were led into a plane hangar. It was bigger than ten football fields! It was also filled with many different planes. Paul and Tom were drawn to a plane much smaller than the rest. It looked like the runt of the litter!

"What's this plane?" Tom asked.

"Meet Spaceship One!" said Pilot Jeffries. "It was the first ship to leave Earth's atmosphere piloted by a civilian. If not for this ship, space travel would still be something only the government could do."

The students' space plane was outside the hangar. It was much larger than Spaceship One.

"Let's go!" Wendy said excitedly. Paul slowly trudged behind her. He wasn't sure about this.

The cabin was as big as the inside of an airplane but with fewer seats. The chairs looked comfortable. Covering each seat was mesh netting made of strong, elastic threads.

"I call the window seat," Wendy said, just as she plopped herself down.

Paul connected the buckles on his harness. He was strapped into the seat.

"Ok, everybody," said a voice from the ceiling. "This is Pilot Jeffries up in the cockpit. We're ready to go, so I'll ask all crew members to take their seats. Is everyone ready?"

No! I'm not ready! Paul thought. This was a dream and he needed to wake up! A cheer rose from the students as they felt the plane begin to move. It rolled slowly at first, but began picking up speed quickly. Paul shut his eyes.

Paul could hear the engines working hard to lift the plane off the ground. He felt like someone was pushing him back into his seat, gently. Then, all of a sudden Paul felt his stomach drop. He gasped, and his hand grabbed at the armrest next to him.

"We're not on the ground anymore!" Wendy told Paul. "Ow! My ears just popped."

After a few minutes, the plane was flying straight again, and the voice of Pilot Jeffries returned.

"That was the easy part," he said. "Now, your seats will retract, and you'll just hang by the netting for this next part. We have to use powerful rockets to escape the Earth's gravity. Otherwise, you'd be crushed against your chair!"

Suddenly, there was the sound of hidden machines whirring! Paul saw the seats in front of him slowly fold into the floor. Then his seat folded! Everyone was now resting in the nets! They were attached to the ceiling and to the floor, but they didn't look too stable to Paul!

"Hang on!" said Pilot Jeffries. "We're about to begin our orbit of Earth!"

There was a loud roar. Paul felt a rumbling all through his body as the main rockets flared. The net stretched and Paul felt like he was being curled into a ball. He felt heavier than usual.

The roar and rumble of the rockets died out, and there was a strange silence. Paul suddenly felt as if he didn't weigh anything at all! He was sure if he left his seat, he would fly away!

"I feel strange!" Paul said. He looked at Wendy and laughed. Her hair was flying!

"Neat!" said Wendy, "Everything floats! We're weightless!"

Just then, Pilot Jeffries opened a door at the front of the cabin, and floated into the cabin. "How's everyone doing?" he called. "You all feel weightless right? Like you're just floating!"

"I feel like I'm on a roller coaster," said Tom from his net. "Like we just went up a steep climb on the tracks, and now we're coming back down. This is so cool!"

"You're not far off, son," replied Jeffries. "You see, what you're feeling now is basically the same thing, just on a larger scale.

"On the roller coaster, you feel like you might float out of your seat," said Pilot Jeffries. "That's because your body and the roller coaster are falling at the same rate of speed. Here in space, the same thing is happening. We're constantly falling back towards Earth. The weightless feeling we have now is because our bodies are falling at the exact same speed that the space plane is falling."

"We're falling?" asked Paul worriedly. "How can we fall out here in space?"

"Well, the space plane travels so fast that by the time it should have fallen to Earth, the Earth has curved away from it," said Pilot Jeffries. "That's what we call an orbit, and it means that until some force moves us, we'll keep circling the Earth. Does anyone know why we are falling back toward Earth?" he continued.

"Gravity!" Wendy called out.

"And what's gravity?" the pilot asked.

Wendy look embarrassed. "Um, I forgot," she said. *Me, too,* thought Paul.

"Maybe we need a demonstration," Pilot Jeffries said. He floated down the aisle and began unfastening the students from their nets. As soon as he did, they floated freely!

"Whee!" Tom called out, and he did a back flip!

Paul felt cautious at first. He gripped onto the edge of the net so he wouldn't fly away! Paul found that floating there, his stomach did not feel as bad as before. Suddenly, he let go of the net and floated across the room. This was fun!

"So, back to gravity," the pilot began again. "Gravity is what makes you fall. It is really much more than that, however. Gravity is a force that causes any two objects to be attracted to each other. Your body is pulled to Earth by gravity, and that is why you fall.

"But gravity works between any two objects in the universe," he continued. "So it attracts the moon to Earth. It also attracts Earth and other planets to the sun. Gravity is present everywhere in the universe, so we say it is universal."

"Does gravity have the same force everywhere in the universe?" asked Paul.

"Nope!" said Pilot Jeffries. "That force depends on how far apart the objects are. If they are far apart, there won't be much pull. But if they are close together, look out! It also depends on what we call the mass of each object."

"The mess?" said Paul.

"The *mass*!" said Pilot Jeffries. "That's how much matter is in something. The more mass an object has, the greater its gravitational force."

"But, how do we know about gravity? How was it discovered?" asked Wendy.

Sir Isaac Newton described gravity.

Before Jeffries could answer, Tom said, "Newton invented gravity! An apple fell on Newton's head! That's when he thought up gravity."

"Sir Isaac Newton was the first to write a formula for gravity," explained the pilot. "He also watched the planets and figured out that some force must be keeping them in their circular motion. He thought it might be the same force that made an apple fall to Earth! That force is gravity!"

"Before I go back to work," continued Pilot Jeffries, "Look out the cabin window."

Paul's mouth dropped open in wonder. There, below them was the Earth! It was a brilliant blue globe. "It's beautiful!" Paul whispered.

"Look! The moon!" Tom cried.

Looking out the cabin window, Paul could see the moon's surface, its gray landscape broken by craters and mountains. There was a man-made dome sitting alongside a rille, or trench. It was a moon base! Spotting people trudging along in their bulky spacesuits, Paul felt a thrill of excitement.

Suddenly there was a bump. Paul's eyes flew open! He was back in the school bus, in front of his school. "I experienced weightlessness!" he thought. "And now I understand gravity! Someday, I'm going to go to the moon for real!"

Sir Isaac Newton

Sir Isaac Newton lived in England during the last half of the 1600s. Although not a very good student in his youth, he became a brilliant man who made important discoveries in the areas of mathematics and science.

Newton created a new kind of advanced math, called calculus. He also studied light. He proved that white light is made up of other colors. You can see what he meant if you let light shine through a glass prism. The prism separates light into all of its colors! Try it and see.

Newton is really known for his work in physics. In his Three Laws of Motion, he described how things move. 1. If you put an object in motion, it will keep moving unless another force acts on it. This means if a ball comes your way, it will keep moving unless you catch it, or gravity pulls it down. 2. Gravity is at work everywhere in the universe. (This is called the Law of Universal Gravitation.) 3. For every action there is an equal but opposite reaction. This means when you sit on your chair, you push down on the chair, but the chair actually pushes up on you. That's why you stay put! In addition, Newton gave us mathematical formulas for measuring the force of gravity.